MW01104777

After Paradise

After Paradise

Janis Rapoport

SIMON & PIERRE

After Paradise

Copyright © 1996 by Janis Rapoport

All Rights Reserved. No part of this publication may be reproduced, stored in a retrieval system, or transmitted in any form or by any means, electronic, mechanical, photocopying, recording, or otherwise (except brief passages for purposes of review) without the prior permission of Simon & Pierre Publishing Co. Ltd. Permission to photocopy should be requested from the Canadian Reprography Collective.

Simon & Pierre
A member of the Dundurn Group

Publisher: Anthony Hawke
Printer: Metrolitho
Front Cover Illustration: "Hallucination" by Hag, used by permission.

Canadian Cataloguing in Publication Data

    Rapoport, Janis
       After paradise

Poems.
ISBN 0-88924-272-0

I. Title.

PS8535.A76A77 1996   C811'.54   C95–931123–8
PR9199. 3. R36A77 1996

Publication was assisted by the **Canada Council,** the **Ontario Arts Council** and the **Book Publishing Industry Development Program** of the **Department of Canadian Heritage.**

Care has been taken to trace the ownership of copyright material used in this book. The author and publisher welcome any information enabling them to rectify any references or credit in subsequent editions.

Printed and bound in Canada

Simon & Pierre	Simon & Pierre	Simon & Pierre
2181 Queen Street East	73 Lime Walk	1823 Maryland Avenue
Suite 301	Headington, Oxford	P.O. Box 1000
Toronto, Ontario, Canada	England	Niagara Falls, N.Y.
M4E 1E5	OX3 7AD	U.S.A. 14302-1000

Acknowledgments

Some of the poems in this book have appeared in the magazines *Nimrod* (U.S.) and *Room of One's Own*, in the League of Canadian Poets' contest anthology *Vintage '94* and in *Border Lines: Contemporary Poems in English*. Some of the poems have appeared in translation in *Revue Europe* (Paris, France).

The author wishes to thank Edward Chamberlin, Douglas Donegani and Renata Donegani for their editorial suggestions.

The assistance of the Ontario Arts Council, through a Works-in-Progress Grant, and of the Canada Council is gratefully acknowledged.

Lines from Gwendolyn MacEwen's "The Grand Dance" are from *Afterworlds* and are used by kind permission of the Canadian Publishers, McClelland & Stewart, Toronto and by Gwendolyn MacEwen's estate.

Author's photograph is by Julia Seager.

This book is in memory of Joshua Julian Barnes (1972-1991).

Contents

Borders

. . . at the edge we see familiar things end and something else begin, something which makes us try to recall another state of being.

— William Irwin Thompson
The Time Falling Bodies Take To Light

Beach

Time is unmade here at the border
of rock and sky. Under brindled water the hours
hide, fall away, disappear with the salt
until you are unknown, unthought, unformed.

There is only pale wind and pearl mist
that lights the granite and the slow green meadows
by the sea. What rite can re-form, re-make,
return you from water, from sand, from the low
dark leaves of a fruit bush pocked with rust?

We hear the echoes of sunbathers who last season
wore only shadows themselves yet laughed at a woman
who drove all the way out from town
to lie naked among strangers.

Unwanted kelp flowers on the cold stone shore.
Somewhere near: hosta, wild roses, morning glories
call out your name. In the perpetual sky
the sun and the moon are still. You don't answer,
you can't. Or else we can't hear you,
the unsinging, the unspeaking, the unliving.

We remain on the beach, ignoring the tide.
You're here, we understand that, and you're happy.
We're at a summer border of ourselves,
of each other, our small chiselled histories.

The moon is monitoring the water, listening
to its incoming waves, asking each white pulse
to unchart and undo our unknowing.

Falling Water

My mother said
find someone else to love her, my son;
somewhere the name of her husband is already written
under falling water on a speckled stone.

She'll want to sit in a meadow, afraid
of what my mother has told her about him,
someone who sleeps among thistles
and small yellow flowers. Son, my mother said,
lead them to each other while he's swimming,
Neither he nor she will be able to see you.

She's wearing blue, one breast covered only
by her hair. There are baskets near her ankles
on the stone ledge where she's squatting.
Someone else is already there in a mask swimming
beneath the waterfall in a dark swirl
just above the rapids. She isn't watching him,
even though my mother said she would.

What she has to do, my mother said,
is gather seeds and sort them, grain by grain.
There's *danger* scrawled in ink on signs
around the waterfall. And *do not descend.*
In her hands are skeins of pure Merino wool.
She's speaking with the white pools
as they spiral around her toes.

A webbed foot surfaces, as if he's found
what he's been looking for in the accelerated water
tucked perhaps among polished moss and stones.
She is also looking, not just because my mother said.

She may never see me yet she tosses
some seeds into the flurry of summer.
And I catch them.

Public Gardens, Halifax

A stone Cupid rides a whale in a grove
of rhododendrons, weigela and weeping elm.
He is waiting for Psyche to sort wheat
from barley from oats and to gather
gold from the backs of absent sheep.
Psyche is pouring the dark water
of her reflection over Cupid's wings
and the backs of whales.
Dead fish lie, like coins, at her feet.
And the rain scrawls taboos
across her stone forehead and her cheeks.

Purcell's Cove

There's a ribbon of mist in front of the trees
on the far side of the harbour. It passes
through sailboats and wraps gulls scanning for food.
A foghorn groans from up the coast
across bird shrieks and engines. The ribbon spreads
toward the city, binding the grey water
to the grey sky.

A click of the camera can't take the rest
of this picture: we too are wrapped in damp spice
and the tang of the sea, our summer faces on the dock.
Shall we eat fog sandwiches?

Purcell's Pond

Under our naked feet, between soft city toes:
red crumble of summer: dead branches, cones, needles, mud.
We trip over rocks, roots, a crust of fallen leaves
rendered by mouths of insects into aromatic lace.
We're protected from the worst by moss tough as stars.
Cicadas flare from secret nests and crickets
scale their voices for the opera of the afternoon.
Dragonflies knit the filigree of their wings
into the blue air. Under such dark water
they say nothing lives.

We watch a child slither down a boulder,
then glide beneath the heavy surface of the pond.
Through the splashes she makes, her pastel arms
filter to rust. A web of currents
cradles this swimmer toward the opposite shore.
Her small body shrinks into a miniature
we could wear around our necks.

The pond dimples with a pant of wind. Might we see
crowned serpents hatch from underwater eggs of stone?
Their wings could mash the surface into waves,
their mouldy breath or glance drown the swimming child.
Such creatures have been sighted here
only in the minds of visitors such as ourselves
who have viewed fossilized basilisk tracks and barbed tail drags
in museums, on beaches and for sale in shops.

Tourist At Parrsboro

From the red beach we can almost see the islands
Glooscap flung down as mudballs in anger
when Beaver tried to thwart his power. That's where
I want to be, walking toward them through terra cotta mud
while you look over here for dinosaur tracks
even smaller than the prints you found before.

What about the roadsigns? you say. I have to confess:
your visitor, doing the driving, has been watching the ground.
You tell me those islands are too far to reach
between tides. Everyone around here knows that.
But locals don't talk to tourists so the same warning's
on the signs. Endorsed by Glooscap himself?
I want to know. Or did he just jab in some posts
as a bit of landscaping after he threw the mud? Did he then
carve warnings in a language he couldn't understand?
His legs, you note, were much longer than ours, his feet
too big for shoes. He was much faster, more secure.
He could walk above the highest tides.
For him those islands were just a few footsteps away.

I start pulling fragments of rock from the cliff.
You're already too far down the beach to notice
prehistory breaking between my hands. There's probably
a sign somewhere about that too, with letters drizzled
around in the air. You've left the food hamper with me
so I pull and walk, walk and pull, kick a few stones,
hurt my foot. I don't even know what I'm looking for.

Just as I'm getting hungry I can't see you anywhere.
But your pick clamours against some rock
and your invisible voice offers a raincoat
in reconciliation. If I refuse I think it means
we'll spend less time here and more figuring out
how to access Glooscap's islands. As usual I'm wrong.
You accept my decision and tell me to go ahead
and eat without you. I squeeze rain from the bread,
wipe the surface of the cheese, puncture wet beads on the fruit.

After my lunch you loom spectral from the fog. I think
you are smiling. Suddenly I want to be alone again,
cut off forever by the inevitable tide. But we leave
what remains of the vanishing beach just in time,
sky and sea lashing at our bodies.

In town there's a statue of Glooscap, skin the colour
of the red sand you've been digging, hair darker
than rainclouds, black eyes staring at those islands of his,
now just about completely underwater. Eyes black with happiness,
or rage? You don't answer. Between Glooscap's legs
there's a mineral museum and store whose sign boasts
miniature dinosaur footprints, the smallest
on this planet. Except maybe those you found this morning.

While I'm looking at quartz crystals, agates and rhodochrosite
as well as the world's reputedly tiniest tracks
the proprietor says the surface of the rock you've brought
is nothing but scratches. He's trembling, sallow, he complains
of the 200 tourists a day and reporters
from the *National Geographic* who know
little about beavers and native mythology,
even less about dinosaurs.

Still want to visit Glooscap's islands? you ask
as we emerge from the museum between his legs. I look
at what you're holding between your hands. The tracks
are shorter and thinner, smaller than those in the shop.
Scratches — yes — made by some of the first
and smallest feet to walk along any shore
before almost anything else stepped out of a shell,
before anger or regret, before power, before.

Parrsboro: Looking For Fossils

In late summer mist, through red sand you dig
toward the past. It's there all right, in something
that had four thick toes with untrimmed claws and huge
and probably scaly feet. You're having trouble
locating just the right seam of rock where prehistory
will be able to respond to the articulate voice of your hammer.

I've been looking up at the cliffs, trying to understand
how they used to jut at another angle, while still rudiments
long ago and undersea. Wave prints in stone and
almost vertical now hang above, over what today is beach.
Sand furrows beneath my cold white feet,
under quick water becomes smooth and flat again.
Tides retreat, recording no pattern of movement
over transparent and almost noiseless surfaces.

They say the daily path the water takes
is Glooscap's legacy. And some say it's not only volcanoes
or earthquakes or ice can drain the ocean, then imprint
and overturn the sand to a precipice instead of beach.
In the soft flesh of the cliff I find something
dark, hard, bright. Jewels belonging
to Glooscap's grandmother are scattered along this shore.
Whatever it is I replant in the damp rock, reaching high
between the bursts of daisies and small, pink roses.

Meanwhile you've given up on the stone footprints.
Your face, your hair are opalescent with rain. Tides will wash
and cover wherever you thought those four-toed feet
clawed among the rockfall. Sand will keep sifting
through the meshwork of time. And you
continue hammering and calling out to whatever
lived here, and died, by its perfect though unremembered name.

Blue Beach

for Don Domanski

Stone beneath slate beneath shale: blue shingles scattered
over the red sand. In your knapsack you carry
whatever it is you'll need. We watched as you packed
a hammer and a spike. This is your beach
and you warn us to be careful.

We've arrived by a steep path studded with blueberries
and wild daisies. It's the only way down and now
the cliff we see above is delicate,
its once prominent profile altered by the fist of time.

A swoop of plovers speckles the sky:
150,000 of them according to your friend.
They stop for shrimp at a sandbar.

Along the shore we find bark, cones, spores.
They have been here for 350 million years,
insect prints, tail drags, the sand they moved on then
now rippled into stone. And amphibian tracks:
three-toed, five-toed, large.

While your friend hunts for bones or fossil eggs
we are told not to discuss the mating habits
of these beached plovers, or the lizards and geckoes,
iguanas and turtles and snakes he keeps
until he can hatch or rejuvenate a brontosaur.

You've got a crowbar under your rubber poncho;
in your hand a brass microscope. The distant
blue shape of your body kneels down among the plovers,
semi-palmated we are later told. They are devouring shrimp
apparently in order to double their weight.

It's hard work on this beach, we already know,
extracting prehistory from immoveable boulders
and rocks jammed into the sand. Scrawls
and glyphs etch their stubborn surfaces.
What is written? And in what code?

In the jaw of the overhang under the dangle
of tree roots and spiders, I think of the slant
of time, how it's angled into these cliffs.
You're at the other end of the beach,
still kneeling, still small.
But I hear the slag of your voice.
Or you're throwing stones. The words are hard rain.

The cliff is falling, exposing more fossils. You're happy,
though not particularly that I'm underneath.
With each rockfall there is more for you to pry out,
more to split open, more to shove
under the impatience of that brass microscope.

Should you ever disappear, perhaps from this very beach,
under an avalanche of roots and stone,
your reptile-collecting friend has asked
that you bequeath him whatever it is
you're looking for today.

A black dog runs down to the shore,
barks at the still feasting plovers. By the time
her companions, the bird watchers, arrive
the birds have flown out over the incoming tide.
The quick march of the water locks all those stories
in the stone once again, carefully drowning the secrets
whose ciphers you will never know
but always desire.

Clam Harbour

Ribbons of sea life crunched yellow under our feet
as we walked along the beach on stones
as oval and as smooth as eggs.

In the shallow meadows above the water
grizzled slugs chewed away on berries
until dragonflies scooped and swallowed
their slow, soft winding.

Back on the sand clamshells didn't want to open.
There was nothing but danger in the salt air.
Periwinkles gripped their driftwood even harder
while water blankets slipped from their unsuspecting bodies
and back into the sea. A long veil of mist paraded,
dividing sand from sand from air from water.

In the dunes insects churred and
a woman lifted a metal rod that struck
an egg or a stone or a shell. Her throat
unravelled in birdsong while a perfect sphere
whirred across blue daisies, among mosquitoes,
above dune thistles and through the blind
and silent damp.

Boreal

for Sara Seager

We begin again in mud, stinking up to the knees.
Our frame is a low fir forest. In the distance
dove-coloured rivers drain away from the horizon.

What journey hasn't begun near a river
in a world whose syllables are joined
through the water-marked palimpsest of bodies?

In the sky thin strips of cloud are indicators for the weather.
We watch their reflection, knowing that we cannot put our feet
even once into the same water. The wind is from the south,
helpful, we are told, for crossing the lakes
and narrow channels that are their inbetween.

The first water coils in long white traps
over precambrian granite plates.

On a remote shore what used to be log tents tilt
into late-summer grass, roofs open
to wood lice and common snipes.

Remains of a silo welcome garbage
under a dome that has collapsed. Later,
segments of a logging barge, trapper's cabin and
snowmobile skeleton, with lawn and toilet seat.

Away from the water, spindly custodians of birch
inscribe the history of the forest in dappled scrolls.

Once: a flock of masked waxwings passing hunted berries
and blossoms along a row of bronze feathers, on a branch.

I'm watching your long and naked back as your paddle dips
and does not dip into indigo water.

The sun is as big as my hand, a seamless jigsaw of fire.
And the water beneath us flows toward a destination
it cannot know, gathered here into a thin stream of our thinking.

Water is death for earth, yet here even our souls become wet.
What we see and catch we leave behind; what we do not see
we take away, engraved into skin or through ears and eyes.

Down and down the river now banked with rust-stained cliffs
and caves sacred to the Cree. Caribou and lynx in petroglyphs:
bait for travellers who fish. Our catch is coveted
by spirit paddlers in miniature stone canoes.

A painted lynx sends spines from its arched back into windthrow
over quick water. In silhouette a lizard kindles sky fire,
hurls loud javelins of rain. Lizards are also for love,
for cures and for luck, especially a lizard held in the hand.
Cave lizards are orange messengers and guides for souls
should we lose ours now to afterworlds.

Beneath this canopy of rock you place and do not place
your thin hand into the same river. You are and you are not.

Beyond the blue and green of the boreal shore
a fringe of spruce and larch conceals an inner band
of sumach, winterberry, rhodora: thick waxy rings
for a circular target whose dark centre is a tea-stained pond.
This bog is archive of pollendrift, seedshed, featherfall,
and of secrets from voyagers unquietly surrendered.

The sky begins its slow bleed into the water.
A bear paw stamps shore mud with shadow.

Over an island of blueberries, the moon on its back
sliced by the sun's rays to the length of an eyebrow.
Can each river have its own moon? I ask.
You answer with a question. You want to know
why I've portaged and paddled so far to be nowhere.

I'm where we are for the unswept needles of spruce
and curled bark of the birch, and for what is written
in loops of sunlight underfoot in the forest. I'm here
for the agile water that carries us through this random voyage
of our imaginations. Here, for the civilization of marshes
and bogs that do not change. I'm here
for the luminous morphology of the moon.

Your spine stiffens along mine, in the tent.
Please stay on your side, I say,
so you cannot see me sleep.

There is a lantern spawned from a marsh or bog
whose light carves demons into the dark. I wear
the mask of my ancestors and parade with them
through a market of altars. Skeletons, skulls
and candied corpses are for sale. This is my dream.
Pottery animals guard the entrance to the moon
where I'm not allowed unless I choose to stay. I offer
the borrowed lantern, my crown of candles and a bouquet of sedge.
The night is incense strung with false Solomon's seal.
I'm wearing a costume of marzipan and red baneberry.
My shawl is trimmed with mirrors. Shaking bells
in celebration of a cosmos that trades neither at a profit
nor at a loss, the moon becomes an anaemic priestess.
She closes the cycle of creation.

You are standing at some distance in our river,
drinking from a cracked white porcelain cup,
bordered by weeds and a marsh beyond my knowing.

Kingfishers rattle the sky. We are unable to trap
the north wind or waves that vault into our canoe.
Yesterday's calm is an unrendered echo, terrain dense
with ruptured memory. We cannot think back, cannot predict.
Today's universe is a white splatter whipped across faces,
an irrational breath holding us still in its shallow mouth,
then dragging us closer and closer to shore.

Advancing from the riverbank, a herd of humpback boulders.
As they swim, a plume of wet netting snares the faint blue air.

The chasm we portage is a neck of churling foam
snagged on claws of stone. This is and is not
the same river now surging between narrow pillars,
its white veins gripped in a perpetual tourniquet:
hydromancer, ready for battle.

You are submerged in the same pulse of growling water
that charms me to the dark overhang
of curiosity and unfulfilled desire, of striving,
fury and chance, of that which we have always imagined,
never known. We are tipped into vertigo
by whomever, whatever has conjured us here.

Did you toss river onto earth?
Did you mix sky with water?
Did you dip a bough of spruce or lizard's tail and say a prayer?
Did you grind white quartz into cloud stones?
Did you dance a ceremonial circle?

Insects stab at our flesh while a loon wails from its red gullet.
The sky is a turquoise jar brimming with chilled rain.

We lie under the open eye of night, each woven into the fabric
of our separate dreams. In sleep I see you again in the river.
You're gliding across rapids, holding a bow
shaped like a lyre. Stretched back on itself
its sinew holds the symmetry of sky. All night
I walk across a bridge of arrows.

To the north is interglacial peat, and gravel islands.
Above them sandhill cranes leap and bow,
extend their wings and feet. A tributary adds
its silty flow, sculpts caverns deep into gypsum
along the shore. The border of land recedes. Tides
from an inland sea, and spirit paddlers in their stone canoes,
pull us forward into the white throat of a horizon
transparent with wind and cross-currents of stars.

We drift and we do not drift downstream.
And in the dreams we do not dream
we are, and we are not.

In the Carousel
of Space

I am simply trying to track you down
In preworlds and afterworlds
And the present myriad inner worlds
Which whirl around in the carousel of space.

— Gwendolyn MacEwen, *Afterworlds*

More Metaphors
(with apologies to Sylvia Plath)

I'm a poem with nine lines,
a kitten, a doll's house,
small cantaloupe with vines.
O ripe melon, jewel, birchbark canoe.
This small round of dough, a brioche in your oven.
The coin, damp with gold, clings to its large purse.
I'm the end of the means, wrapped in cellophane.
You swallowed yellow mangoes or bullets
on a train without space for acrobats.

Ivory

The heart's winter breath
plucks at bare apple branches:
ice-woven lovesongs

Pewter

A pearl mist curving
through the marshlands of April:
signature of peace

Amber

Van Gogh's stars are eggs:
menu at the night café.
In our dark mouths, fire

Gossip *Ragoût*

Gossip, like poetry, cannot usefully be defined.
　　—(*précis*) Patricia Meyer Spacks, *Gossip*

Gossip is best prepared in an atmosphere of intimacy, warmth
and bonding, and in the absence of any intended victims.

Into a large bowl place a pound of secrets,
real or imagined, and of varying sizes.
Mix with a pint of fantasy, a cup of speculation,
a teaspoon of innuendo and a dash of malice.
Marinate for several days, turning frequently,
adding dialectic as required.

Remove the secrets with a slotted spoon
in order best to separate the marinade.

Simmer the reserved marinade for additional flavour
with a chunk of apprehension streaked with ambiguity.

Combine with the secrets, then cover
and simmer again, until tender.
Add a touch of jealousy and a few stalks of rumour.

Remove the secrets to a platter of suspicion.

Thicken the sauce that remains with speculations,
half-truths and ambitions, mixed with an ounce or so of scandal
so that there will be ample for each serving.

Pour the sauce over the secrets.

Sprinkle with flakes ground from a rumour mill.
Garnish with elaborations, attractively arranged.
Spread sprigs of slander on top.

Serve with the inside scoop in absolute privacy
initially to close friends and confidants,
being sure to save some as a surprise for the victim(s).

There is always an appetite for gossip:
it impels plots and drives narratives.

Some of its consumers may enjoy gratification
of previous or current — and voracious — envy or rage
while others may experience acute indigestion,
though the consequences of feasting on gossip
cannot exactly be calculated and often cannot be controlled.

In some parts of Africa dining on gossip is considered a delicacy
after which the lips of the diners are severed from their mouths.

In North America gossip *ragoût* is eaten regularly:
its shadow reputation endures; scars mark its victims,
although gossip itself may be transient, invisible, ephemeral,
whether vanishing or emerging from throats, from kitchens,
or from the intimate spaces between imagination and deceit.

A Ceremony of Oysters
for Tony Houghton

Above the terrace that is your garden, the dawn
drifts down in fine, blue grains
and joins dark insects in the spicy earth.

Beneath the nimbus of an avocado tree, vibrato of jasmine.
Camellias are about to blossom in the only colour
they can remember: *California softshell cha cha pink*.

From narrow branches, columns for small dark leaves,
I harvest a cluster of oranges and devour them all
in your terra cotta kitchen before you come downstairs.

This is the only fruit you desire, the only fruit
your tree will bear all year. You wouldn't have told me,
as the guest of your new wife, had I not asked.

An advertising executive or an alchemist could dissolve
the pulp from my throat or stomach, suck the nectar
from my hollow blood, borrow the colour from tomorrow's sunrise

and return the oranges to the table, or the tree. But we'd both
have to believe in more than the solemn mauve of the patio orchid
or the lemon-coloured stars trailing over mossy bricks

and under the ripening of your arbour. We'd have to believe
in the severing of time and in the hanging face of the stone lion
whose sculpted surfaces my morning fingers traced

in anticipation of the *lustre* of your *classically inspired* car,
triumph of judicious and harmonious technology, taking us
— *in the embrace of leather* — over a saffron-coloured bridge

named for the sun or perhaps for coins
placed in the mouths of the ancient dead or
something radiant: prosperity or heaven.

This is the bridge. This is the bridge that did not break
when the earth moved and water swallowed the earth
that swallowed water. And the water laughed

shifting its undersea volcanoes, one of our last
unexplored frontiers. Is this what we deserve?
A pageant of seaweed, thorns and barnacles

across the shore while ocean tectonics remain
as unmapped as the icons of memory between us,
roads to your house, skyways, vineyards;

as unchartable as unseasonable weather and
the next earthquake, as unpredictable as the water
under the other bridge that broke apart,

surrendered its cold and wet amorphous heart
to oracles or molecules and quarks. I'm thinking
of your daughters, how they will live

and those of your young wife. They're all called Miranda.
I hear them breathing into their instruments.
Each has chosen an aulos: ionian, dorian, phrygian.

When you come downstairs to only the pocked fragments
of your precious fruit; when you come downstairs
before Sausalito, Mill Valley, the bridge over all that water

which will take us there in a car with *electronic links*
in *dynamic balance*, you reach for the glass doors, only glass
that separates us from the garden, the terrace,

tendrils of shadow; only glass while you ask
about the difference between an advertisement and a recipe,
a recipe and a poem. While you're out there dancing

on the young moss, thinking how you'll reconceive
each level of the garden, someone cuts the clouds.
A swath of peacock falls, then disappears.

I stay behind glass, in the kitchen, to gild a soufflé
of poems. You eat and enjoy your breakfast without tasting
any words. You don't — you can't. The delicacy

of sound or shape glides past your teeth
in the early light. I'm inhaling the pink of the hibiscus,
the white of the star magnolias while I ask

for clarification of what you mean by the difference
between a good recipe, a good ad, a good poem.
You've already swallowed all the metaphors.

What has vanished? What remains? You leap onto the patio,
put your face beside the stone lion's, open your mouth
in the same perfect oval, wait for a tide of shadow, or rain.

Poetry isn't about words, you say. It's what you hear, touch:
it's energy, mazes, change. So is advertising.
So is food. So is art. You stay there, crouched,

your grey curls hardening to grey stone scrolls,
your breath circular. When your wife calls out
to your daughters who are Miranda, each playing on her aulos:

lydian, mixolydian, locrian, you'll drive us
in a *traction controlled system* over the bridge named
for metal and coin, to Mill Valley, Sausalito, Alcatraz

in the *sanctuary* of your *multi-linked suspension* car. I'll sit
on the roof, not far from *platinum-tipped sparkplugs*,
performing a ceremony of oysters, co-opting them

from advertisements and the watery arch of their homes,
for the recipe that has become this poem, promising them
liberty if not life among zinnia elegans and lavendar verbena,

offering *an emotional rebate* through improved accommodation
among white and yellow poppies. In the ageless afternoon
your garden will be photographed for a magazine ad:

the stone lion, the small ooze of your morning footprints
now drowning in sunlight, the newly arrived oysters.
Among lilies and peonies, lamps of rhododendrons
your camera-ready daughters will perform an aeolian sonata.

The Knives of Tabitha Calipso

Words pass between us with the yowl
of the sharpening of knives. Narrow and silver
they pull back the skin of a scalp
to expose the fruit of a brain.

I search for the blades that are next,
those syllables unspoken among the dark coils
at the back of your neck but your hair,
damp with summer, isn't talking tonight.

Yet you pulled loudly on mine until filaments fell,
strand by strand, finally silenced
into spirals on the bleached white
cotton of your pillow.

A pillow for sleeping, now dissected by moonshadow
and the crescent leap of a millennium cat
whose night voice tangled the bedroom curtains
above an open window sill

while knives red with our blood
retold the promise and the brindle
long ago engraved through air torn with fire
into the darkening opus of her name.

Canis Candens: Celestial Canine

A blind dog walks along a path of cloud. Beneath him a lagoon
spreads long tentacles of damp. Someone he cannot remember, a
woman perhaps, once a white-haired companion, has named him
guardian of the lagoon. A hand scatters some hard yellow seeds.
They dent his tangled fur. The dog keeps walking. He is higher
now, well above the planet. His is an elliptical orbit, the perimeter
of a large insect. He keeps on walking. Stars form at his feet. A
voice calls out, asking him not to forget the summer solstice and to
protect the reaping of what has been sown. He walks, through sky
lion and dot-to-dot swan, past eagle and lyre. One of the yellow,
pitted seeds has swollen, risen high into the air, as large and flat as a
plate. A white-haired woman waits for him. She is shadow but he
knows her. She is cooking chicken soup. And he stops to sniff that
familiar, fragrant vapour before it too thins into cloud, sky water,
rain on earth lagoons and dark insects, swimming.

At the Horse Races: Breeders' Cup Day

Boots 'n' Jackie Fight for Love in *Secret Odds* at *Devil's Rock*.

It's *A Li'l Known Fact Jolypha Corrupts Doctor Devious
Living Vicariously* as *Marling* or sometimes the *Magical Maiden*,
even *Queen of Triumph*.

Defensive Play at *Salt Lake* lures *River Special*
into a *Firm Pledge* with *Zoonaqua*. *They'll Set Them Free*
under the *Versailles Treaty* at the *Harbour Club*
while *Beal Street Blues Exchange Subotica* with *Trishyde*.
Theirs is a *Twilight Agenda*.

At *Navarone* a *Sea Hero Strolling Along* in *Gilded Time*
takes an *Educated Risk* with a *Culture Vulture*
called *Señor Speedy*.

Meafara and her *Mountain Cat* have a *Tactual Advantage*
in the *Sudden Hush* by the *Lotus Pool*.

Meanwhile *Luthier Enchanteur* on the *Saratoga Dew
Exits* to *Nowhere . . . Furiously*.

There's a *Brief Truce* at *Paradise Creek* when *Rubiano*
watches *King Corrie* do a *Turkstand* on a *Creaking Board*.

But *Eliza* and *Liberada*, the *Diamond Duo* of *Cardoun*,
take a *Shared Interest* in *Fowda* who wears *Jolie's Halo*
under a *Meadow Star* in the *Life Light*.

Sheikh Albadon thinks he's *Thunder Regent* at the *A.P. Indy*,
a *Fourstars Allstar* like *Rodrigo de Triano* at *Paesana*.
Such a *Pleasant Tap*.

Booly and *Mr. Brooks* hire *Supah Gem* to sing a *Sultry Song*
while they *Quest for Fame* under *Fraise*
and *Reign Road's Technology.*

In *Forty-Niner Days*, *Zoman* and his *Marquetary*
practised *Thirty Serves* on *Arazi* in *Val de Bois*
near *Caponistro* in *Daros.*

With a *Superstrike Elbio* passes *Gray Slewpy* somewhere
between *Selkirk* and *Snowtown.* Or is it *Cardamania*?

It's *Thunder Rumble* in the *Bistro Garden*
when *Love of Silver* in a *Sky Classic* with *Solar Splendour*
Strikes the Gold.

Terrapin

1

Locked beneath the bone fortress of your own body
you search for sand, dig yourself down, exposing only
the dome of your back, and dark birthsong.

Perpetuity is implanted with each eggfall,
each deep, diminutive burial.

When your hatchlings emerge, they'll scrawl
a unique language along the beach
while they skitter toward their first light:
a red fruit suspended
above the abundant salt broth of the sea.

2

We are what we eat — and drink —
according to some medical practitioners,
as we tunnel ourselves out of the past
and into the future:

Take turtle-bone wine for general aches.
Eat an eye to see in a storm.
Boil a section of shell for fever or stroke,
a whole bladder for swelling and pain.
Drops of glandular secretions for heartache.
A front flipper, or claw, for ailments of the liver,
one from the rear if for a spleen.
The tip of a tail, or excrement, for delirium and paralysis.
A testicle or ovary to intensify passion.
The neck to diminish muscle pain, ulcers, convulsions.
An unhatched egg to enrich eyesight or the colour of the blood.

3

You are honoured by those who have seen you dance.
They wear headdresses iridescent with parrot feathers
and sashes sewn with little copper bells.
Bells too for bracelets, anklets, necklaces.
The dancers move sunwise to the beat of gourd rattles
while the wide, blue bands painted on their backs
undulate as a single shorewave just before it shatters.

They celebrate your journey from water to land to air.

4

With a jade-green dragon, phoenix and alabaster tiger
you swim through the cosmos.
Our planet is balanced on your carapace.
You carry prehistory, evolution, fire
as protector of moonrise, starfall and birth.

Into the Peaceable Kingdom
for Adele Wiseman, in memory

A wooden parrot flies on wires, stiff feathers a turquoise fan against
the autumn sun. Above the yellow-green lawn and anonymous
complaints, a blushing plaster pig sings red notes from a Manitoba
maple. She squeals the by-law aria of residential property
maintenance and occupancy standards, practising her song for
bureaucrats and inspectors. Along the open-porch railing stands a
group of illuminated flamingos. They are plastic and pink, glowing
in tentative hope, off and on, on and off. Hum of electric joy. A
civic official from the committee of property standards, summoned
by neighbours he refuses to name, finally agrees homeowners do
have the right of determination for their own décor. So a plaster
tiger from a local store joins the Peaceable Kingdom. His eyes blink
to a syncopated beat. While the left eye lights up red, the right one
is dark. The right eye reddens as the left eye goes out. His
companion is a green-eyed blinking lion, and their on/off rhythm
together is a kind of optical jungle jazz. Nearby a white egret
shines, witness and map of the night. One morning the Inspector
himself arrives, the logic of civic by-laws on his lips. He praises the
concept of renovation but remains suspicious of promises and
verbal contracts. He warns of charges that can be laid, hearings
authorized, summonses, *in-absentia* trials, registered convictions,
fines. He smiles. Ratsy is sent out to negotiate. Ratsy is sometimes
pink or purple, sometimes turquoise, often green. He is luminous,
long-tailed, effervescent, perched on the roof. His rodent teeth
gleam. Into the Peaceable Kingdom a second wooden parrot flies,
stiff feathers, like the first, a turquoise fan against the autumn sun.
A sun that could gather opinions from anonymous neighbours and
process their complaints in the furnace of a kindled eye and let
justice travel down its golden ladders back to earth. Meanwhile the
Inspector retreats to his office in the city and the new parrot joins
the pig still singing in her maple tree where a pale egg appears
among the branches and then another.

An Entomologist and His River

for Henry Frania and Aiya Jurjans

An entomologist sits in a lane drinking tea
with his pregnant wife and a small caged parrot.
They are surrounded by weeds,
tall with summer and rain, and broken fences.
There's a backyard the landlord won't let them use.
How do you like my river? the entomologist asks. You can't
see the fish, yet they're taking the stonefly lures I've provided
just the same.

The parrot looks at himself in a piece of mirror.
The entomologist's wife says the parrot is so bonded
to his own image he won't leave the cage. A book
her husband bought claims self-bonding marks
training stage one. This the entomologist, though busy fishing,
is able to confirm. During stage two or three
or later on such a bird, in captivity, will transfer
the bonding of self to bonding with a person.
He will walk up and down both your arms
and preen the hair on your head into feathers,
using a beak that can puncture stones and a tongue
blacker than bruises or the charring of noise.

While the parrot is in self-training we sit
by the entomologist's river, a strip of cracked asphalt
between banks of weeds and vines,
sipping tea in the August twilight.
This bird is so disillusioned he's stuck at stage one,
still in love with images of himself, not knowing anything
about fishing, not to mention the essence of reflection
or reality, or the difference inbetween. So we sit,
split-bamboo rods in arcs, not catching anything

with our lemon-coloured stoneflies
crafted by the entomologist from live models,
using yellow parrot feathers. So we sit, having to explain
the bonding habits of certain birds to an unborn son.
So we sit, watching our fishing lines pattern the sky.
From the northeast, Perseid meteors start to fall
through city haze and heat. Their brightness tangles
in our hair and through the parrot's outspread wings,
transforms weeds into bulrushes, vines into willow trees.
And for a moment the asphalt ripples into water.
The entomologist holds up what looks like a trout
with dots on its back, radiant
under the incandescence of vanishing skyrocks.

The parrot, skipping a training stage or two, pushes open
the door of his cage, flies off with the trout in his beak.
All around us the sky is open with a silent display
of insects vivid with parrot breast-feathers
luring us to a laneway of fish
just across a river of floating stars.

Gemini

for Elie William Peretz Waitzer
and Benjamin Albert Peretz Waitzer

Twin navigators
through the magic webs of night
snacking on starmilk

The sky your playground
its stars: rungs of bright ladders
dreaming miracles

Astraea, Goddess of Justice

For the height of injustice is to seem just without being so.

—Plato, *The Republic*

At moonrise Astraea starts across the navy sky.
In her right hand, a palm leaf; in her left
an ear of wheat. During certain seasons
the wheat is a weapon and the leaf a pair of scales.

Underneath her crossing a man is thrown
from a moving car into a winter laneway.
His arms and legs are bound with rope, his mouth
shut with reflecting tape. Blood
from his broken face braids the ice.
What remains of his body
has been punched, kicked, shaven, stripped.

The scales Astraea carries darkly
are brimming with starlight, passion,
liberty, honour and faith.

Through the viscous band across his lips
the man's throat burns a bright red circle.
Out of silence he emerges in blotchy, deep *crescendo*.

Astraea listens, her night sky drifting
between thin channels of light, balancing evidence
in the knit of hot coronal winds
and the almost forever shawl of solar gas.

The man in the city laneway knows
he is a victim of those he once attacked,
tied up and robbed. He has already been judged
by others, then jailed behind the vertical dark.

Cloaked in ultraviolet, Astraea advances toward dawn
across transparent canyons of interstellar space,
her scales tilted by earth signals and skytides
among glowing orbits.

Solar Aspects

The sun is a medallion pinned on a blue cloth,
a crown forged through a harvest of heat, a shield
against perpetual dark. The sun is an apple, an apricot,
a peach, a red plum. It's an orange tomato ripening
on a summer vine. The sun is a flower always in bloom,
a single pea in a pod, a cheese bagel, a pancake
on a cosmic plate cooking away in an alchemical kitchen
designed by physicist gourmets. The sun is dessert,
a multi-layered cake of hydrogen and helium, swirled
with scarlet plume icing, accented by burnt-out candles
of stellar ash. Post dessert it's a bright candy looping
along the throat, spiciest against tongue and teeth.
As an eye the sun travels just under Ra's forehead
across the sky in a boat, attended by hawks, scarabs
and rams' horns while vulture wings beat.
The sun is a cell, a spore, a seed, a knot of light
we hope will keep turning. The sun is the rim
of a well, a bucket of wishes, a newly formed stone
shot through Apollo's bow in his pursuit of Niobe.
The sun is music, inspiration and peace, a disc
radiant with prophecy, a gambling chip or coin,
a record we've all forgotten. The sun is a baseball
pitched into the galaxy, a button that dresses
the afternoon, a lamp we use but can't turn off or on.
Under its honeycomb of light Atlas sweats,
lifting the earth on naked shoulders, suspended forever
at the border of night and day. The sun is rouge
on the face of the sky, a mouth feasting on atoms.
The sun marks the end of a sentence with blood,
seals the red roof of tomorrow. The sun is a violet wound,
a tarnished gong that cannot drown.

Ghosts & Angels

τίς δ' οἶδεν εἰ ζῆν τοῦθ' ὃ κέκληται θανεῖν,
τὸ ζῆν δὲ θνήσκειν ἐστί; πλὴν ὅμως βροτῶν
νοσοῦσιν οἱ βλέποντες, οἱ δ' ὀλωλότες
οὐδὲν νοσοῦσιν οὐδὲ κέκτηνται κακά . . . .

Who knows if that which we call death be (not) life,
and life death? . . .

— Euripides, Φρῖξος (*Phrixus*), fr. 830 Nauck

Saltwater Ghosts

1

Through small tongues of water I return to land
by way of the citadel tower and its polished clock face.
There is perpetual damp in this season of fish
though our eyes aren't always summer,
nor our hair. It's so late and wet the tourists are gone;
yet someone is running, scarcely.
And the clock is tocking brine, chronometry.
Underneath that circle of white time
the body of a man reaches. One arm passes through
the brick wall of the tower. On his head is a top hat
streaked with salt. That's next to disappear.
Then coattails. Now I've become the scarce, running sound
but the bricks won't let me follow, and the clock
won't tell me how, or when.

2

Above the citadel polka dots whiten the woven-blue field of sky.
Night is the drift of this flecked tapestry
punctuated by bootsteps heard above, from the ramparts,
their keen drumming striking through our history, our wars
on land or water. These footsteps are joined by others,
by regiments, cotillions of trumpets and bayonets. My heart
beats in synchronicity while the dark sky
convulses cloud and stars. To turn is to see my grandfather
cloaked in the red and gold of high-ranked military.
He inspects me with mulberry stained eyes. There's the curve
of a frown where his forehead used to be. Down the hill
volante over the concise grass of autumn.
In the morning there are reports of murder
under the ramparts of the citadel, gunshot scattered
through the victim's body like pustules of scurvy.

3

Under tar and traffic, civilization squeezed
the citadel water artery between sewer tunnel walls.
The sewer water many still believe to be ideal
for breeding alligators whose eggs have floated
at that location since Mesozoic times.
Through one of these artificial tunnels, they say,
descendants of those eggs pushed a seedling
their mother carried from the south. The seedling
— semi-tropical, seagreen — grew into a hanging tree.
Those condemned to die can still be seen in shadow,
torsos swinging just above the jaws of under-concrete alligators
waiting for verdicts, past or future, whose penalties
are handed down in sinew, flesh or bone.

4

However you look through the glass
there's a profile in the church window of someone
who wants to be admired more than pine timbers
and oak frames, the three-tiered baroque steeple:

Someone who died in an explosion, someone who burned
or drowned, someone perhaps whose spirit wandered
out of a burial vault.

You are asked to change the glass in the window.
The silhouette imprints its line again, during.

5

In an attic room the innkeeper was reluctant to rent
— even though I am a doctor —
a man appears, claims the extra bed.
He has been out drawing and offers me a sketch.
I choose a depiction, in soft pencil, of a young woman
who somehow seems familiar by her hair.
We bolt the door and window,
wish each other well for the night.
By sunrise the artist has gone
though window and door are still bolted.

According to the innkeeper, the young woman
in the sketch given to me by its creator
had been waiting in that same room
for her fiancé, the artist, when he drowned
while trying to render the meaning of tide water.
She's the catatonic I have seen in the asylum.

6

You sleep in a stone room cloistered by stone outer walls.
You have come here for a cure, or to die.

You hear cards being shuffled, then dealt. Feet scrape
across wood, and tap. Goblets hum with wine.

Something heavy pulses on the floor. Voices flare.
You think of fruit slashed from a tree
or an elevated vine drenched in its own essence on the ground.

Moonsheen crinkles through the small window.
The gamblers and dancers are ciphers in light
fragile with discerning. As necromancers they return
whenever you sleep in a stone room, cloistered.

7

Boarders who slept on the painted wooden bed,
in whatever room, complained of unquiet dreams.

A woman would watch the burial of her own body.
She could see right through the casket a carelessness
and temper in herself she had not noticed when alive.

A man might wade through dark water,
never quite reaching the horse-pulled coach
just beyond the harbour.

We slept in the bed ourselves. The night
broke into pieces we could neither repair nor replace.

During a séance the haunted bed spoke: of quarrels and knives,
and body parts submerged beneath a pier. From the carved
and decorated bed we scraped sagacity and paint.
Beneath the paint there was mahogany. Beneath the wood
was blood and a whispering we could almost hear.

Keep the bed and we'd be keeping in perpetuity the suffering
of whoever first dreamt there and died, by knives.
If we destroyed the bed the dreamer,
and the dreamed, might leave.

8

Two men sit in a room at a table.
Someone has dealt cards.

The roof above them forms a cone: elongate, symmetrical.
It is shingled with fish scales the colour of flesh.

For one of the card players the wager is eternity.
The other gambles a soul: his own.

At the front of the house there is a portico
with a small oval window framed in stone.

After this difficult game of cards, a soul separates
from a body, who knows how.

The oval window that displayed in serene reflection
winter and shadows, garlands of slow-moving stars,

is sudden with a struggle and a darkness
whose passage is recorded in its glass.

9

A bartender notices a reflection
he would like to think might be his own, though the image
in the restaurant mirror is somewhat older, bearded
and tattooed with knots and foreign flags.
Fragments of glass, and wood, fall from his hair.
It is past midnight: no more drinks. The bartender turns
to inform the customer, still partly expecting a version
of himself. There isn't anyone sitting behind him left to tell.

Yet in the mirror the man is raising a piece of singed paper:
a schoolchild's spelling list: *thou eternity away forever*.
On the third finger of the left hand he wears naval emblems
embossed onto a brass ring. Beyond his image, scapulars
and a crucifix. There is a web of smoke.

Along the counter toward the crammed ashtrays
the bartender reaches for his future through his past.
Vermilion embers leap from the night. The figure
in the mirror starts to burn, a pocketwatch dangling
from an ear. And on the bartender's cheek,
two red hands: insignia of unidentified intervals,
the unrecorded and the unclaimed.

10

From a replica of his sister's body
a tombstone chiselled out of marble overlooks the sea.

Someone holding a conch shell once waved to him
in the cemetery, speaking only
in unbreathed and unvoiced syllables.

The deceased woman's brother grasped a rake. The rake
passed through the torso of the undead
with whom he had tried to communicate. There was
no muscle, blood or bone.

A woman found her son unclothed, near the sculpture
of her buried daughter, looking out over water.
His body was stippled by tines, with fish tails
scattered where had been his hands and feet.

11

A long white dress drifted just below the surface of the water.
Men, trawling for scallops, reached out for fabric
or for fortune. The dress swam into transparency.
Those fishing, disappeared.

Some people have accused the young woman who wore the dress
on her wedding day, even after her sailor fiancé
had drowned.

Some hold the dress itself responsible, though locked
in an attic trunk for many years.

Others blame the young woman's sister who first wore the dress.
She said the cloth was an aberration of starlight.

12

Women in red jackets emerging from prayer
and the red coats of the military aboard a guardian fleet
held a pirate and his accomplices
between land and further water
simply by the colour of their clothes.

The women on shore and the men navigating a tide
watched small flares appear on the decks between them
before a crew's dreams spun into a vortex of smoke,
and sparking clouds scorched the morning air.

Suspended above water at about the height of a ship's mast
a cluster of red lights often advances
slowly, and alone, toward the harbour.

13

Freighted with cornmeal, raisins, wine
or perfumes, garnets, silk, glass
or settlers, their diaries and books, munitions, a marquis —
a brigantine you could see from the island shore
was stopped by sandhills below water.
Sandhills the captain thought were shadows whose shapes
could clutch a vessel, or let it go. You were
a rescuer in a dory sent against towerings of water
under a sky so crammed with clouds they fell,
revolving with the ocean. You looked down
into a cargo of white clusters, your own skin
emptied of bones, your hair salted and curled.
You drowned in undersea dunes reciting an *aubade* of sand
to a wreath of porpoises and seals.

On other rescues — for the crews of *Triumph* and *Stranger*,
Puritan and *Orpheus* — the dory bowseat is reserved
still for you. The rescued have seen you rise
out of water drained from glaciers to take your place,
grab the oars. You, silent harvester
of shore primrose and stranded sealife,
of weather, meridians, prosperity and change,
of underwater caves collapsed with sand,
of the mirage that has now become our anchor.

14

I've lived on an island almost two hundred years.
Someone sent me here on a ship with ivory coloured sails
and masts carved from red timber. There was a storm.
Isn't that typical? When isn't the water blown
into liquid mountains here? The ship of course disappeared.

Boats with cargoes are always sinking near these island coasts.
Only now instead of stolen gold and ornaments I understand
it's fish and oil they're looking for.

With marooning: the arrival of pirates and their cannons
and swords, or guns. They followed me to shore
where I lay swollen and wet on a night dune, my hand
a beacon with its large bright ring. They didn't cut off
my whole hand only the fourth finger,
coveted for the hard white jewel of love.

No one stays here. Nothing that lived ever returns. And yet
sometime after my drowning a hut appeared. I thought
of my husband or someone sent to find me. I fell asleep
on what in memory resembled a bed, and an animal loped off
through shadow. Whether I was dreaming — can I still dream? —
a man with epaulets tried to speak to me. I don't think
he could hear what I had to say about avarice and lust
or the esteem in which I hold water and the shape
of the sand that is this island as it transmutes
with wind and rain, claiming more
than sunken cargo and myself for history.

15

Sand and water are what I remember,
the slow hard singe against my skin,
the cold penumbra of the sea.
A dune of dark cinders, that was my bed,
yours too, after the bruise of summer
moved you through the funnel of my body.
Birdfeet branded your small spine.
Your newborn limbs I held with the louvres of my hands
as we gathered rice, doused sand with birthwater,
scattered brine through reeds rolled into pipes.
Some hunters, looking for what they could not see,
stole you instead. My arms are a bone cradle
near a whiffle of sand and water. I will walk
until I find you, child. Child, return to me,
rest here, at our island of white birds.
We'll grate feathers into clouds above the beach.

16

My trial will be held in a red chamber
among shells and roses, thistles and acorns
moulded from lime mixed with sand and with water.

All I did was to sail from England with family treasures,
a careful practitioner of plutology.

Under fluted pillars pressed against red walls
they are sprinkling kernels of maize.
They are pouring oil, and wine.

With commands spoken in smooth syllables
foreign pirates overtook the ship, stabbing us
one by one with knives. Scarlet ropes of blood
tangled over the deck: throbbing tapestry, in red.
The ocean broke into jagged canopies and the ship's bow
kept slipping beneath the billows toward a sunset
no one could see. It was me they blamed — after my murder —
for that and for an avalanche of winds, pyramids
of water, an amethyst mirage.

Although already dead, I will sit in the red room
under a white dome festooned with plaster lace,
listening to testimony accusing my ghost
of causing posthumous catastrophes.

Angels

And at her last word every angel sphere
 began to sparkle as iron, when it is melted
 in a crucible, is seen to do down here.

And every spark spun with its spinning ring:
 and they were numberless as the sum of grain
 on the last square of the chessboard of the king.

—Dante Alighieri, *Paradiso*, XXVIII

1

In a north-American city a woman with an Italian name
is handing out angels. They are quite small, and appear to be
crafted from plaster and magenta paint. She is giving them
to churches and street corners, bus stops and walls,
parks, garbage dumps and empty lots,
at ten to the square mile.

The rest of us hang angels on seasonal trees,
imprint cookie dough with their profiles,
dramatize them in novels and pageants, or on TV.
What we imagine to be their likeness we draw, paint, carve.
We subscribe to newsletters, note sightings, participate
in seminars, enrol in courses in divinity. We go out
to buy them in specialty boutiques. Our children,
lying down outside in winter, believe
by moving body parts through piled-up cold white crystals
the shapes they create will rise as angels
from the ground, transformed somehow by sun or wind
or an invisible, related power
whose name was written, earlier, in rain or leaves.

2

Angels of plaster, angels in parks, angels to study,
to eat or admire. Angels of winter, as snow, as wind.
Angels cut out of crystal, folded from paper.
Angels forged from black and red fire.

When you least expect them they appear
even as oxen, even as wolves
with the scaled wings of a griffon
or a peryton's plumed crown.

Even as hoarfish clothed in solitude and tears,
holding splayed dreams between fins.

Sometimes disguised by torsos of serpents and crocodile heads,
mouths that can sing for the sun to appear.
Sometimes with bellies draped in smoke, bellies
disgorging blood onto dark and light squares.

Or sometimes with tails that are water, and carry
sacred pages, scrolled with words, where knowledge
is continually inscribed, in code.

3

We're more used to thinking of angels
as compassionate creatures in invisible places
performing venerable deeds:

Guardians of the entrance to Paradise,
taking a sip of nectar from the Tree of Life;

Protectors of the dawn or of apples
in heavenly gardens, fragrant with truth;

Presiders over virtues, gathering prayers
of the faithful, garlands for the unborn;

Teachers of writing beginning simply,
with thoughts or images in ink on paper;

Witnesses to childhood's bitter sweet
and of the secrets in early knowledge;

Chroniclers of what is good and what is not
from gatherings then, now and after;

Authors of epistemology, earthly and celestial
and of that which can make stars leave the sky;

Jugglers of thunder and terror,
repentance and rain;

Consultants on chalices created from breath,
pouring life's essences
from one small bowl to another, like wine.

4

Some of the more compassionate angels we have (re)created
in our own image(s), expanded or enhanced, according to what
we most fear, or most desire.

There's an angel whose eyes and tongues are said to reflect
all that is alive on our planet. These become dull and diminish
in times of war, holocausts and plagues.

There's an angel with hands and fingers enough
to be always writing the names of those newly born.
These same hands and fingers unwrite the names of those
whose souls divide from their bodies at death.

At the moment of death an angel is witness.
There are rods of silence and promises that burn forever.
To preserve these flames an angel needs four faces
turned toward four corners; for extra support: four wings.

So that all the living are not attacked by fire and heat
an angel receives the first rays every dawn
on spread wings whose purple circles
the arrival of morning in advance of the sun.

The sun and the moon and the sky are held
in the palm of an angel who is thousands of years
taller than any other, an angel robed in clouds,
standing on oceans.

There's an angel with a torso of beryl, and limbs
of polished brass, a face as bright as lightning,
eyes hung with seeing lanterns of fire.
This angel's saffron mouth speaks with all our voices.

Somewhere there's an angel who protects us
with wings woven from substances we cannot know
and colours we do not see.

5

Angels of protection, of fire, of grief,
of clouds and comets, peace and frost.
Angels of terror and time, amulets and air,
of sorcery, vegetables and truth.
Angels of music, of prayer and rain,
of anger and luxury, mountains and zeal.
Angels of pride and perversion, punishment and rage,
of liberty, animals and herbs.
Angels of altitudes, of invention, of joy,
of insolence, confusion and dreams.
Angels of vengeance and aspiration, vindication and the sea,
of scandals, justice and sorrow.
Angels of lust, of oblivion, of dreams,
of gambling and water insects, the zodiac, the apocalypse.
Angels of wind and beginnings, poetry and plagues,
of knowledge, corruption and love.
Angels of appetite and war, hypocrisy and storms.
Angels of the equinox, of the newborn and of silence,
of cooking and art critics, pollen and tongues.
Angels of solitude, of hunting, of the abyss,
of tears and vibration, of science and souls.
Angels of immorality and light, chaos and creation,
of darkness, of blood, of ice.
Angels of islands and healing. Angels of paradise.

6

To conjure most angels, you can call out their names
from the four corners of the world. Your voice
must be as clear as the air at sunrise and more powerful
than the energy in an explosion. Pronounce the angels' names
three times, no more, no less. Your speaking
must be even in length and space. What you say
must then be repeated each by cornetto and sackbut,
dulcimer and lute.

To be successful in romance, wait for the second dawn
after a new moon. Pour the fragrance
from a wild cucumber into a goblet crafted from mist.
Pronounce the name of the angel of love
and the name of your beloved. Write their names
on bark dipped in sunset water, and wait.

To play chess with an angel, use a board
from a tree whose bark is rough, and patterned
with square rings. The board must be made
by someone recently bereaved or one who is very old
and has a connection with the spirits of the dead.
The queen and the king are to be carved
from anomolgus teeth, the pawns
from the placenta of a newborn barometz.

To fulfil ambitions or goals, watch for
the first flicker of the sun at the horizon
on a clear morning when you know the moon
has been full. Weave a carpet
from invisible wool. Go to an island,
where no one else lives, spread the carpet
to the east and to the west. Enclose the carpet,
and yourself, in a sand circle while calling
upon the angels of beginnings and invention.

In your left hand take the point of the carpet
at the east and move it toward the north, west
then south and call the angels of appetite, liberty
and dreams. Fold the carpet, and take it home.

7

It is said we originate from angels, from among those
who couldn't decode evil or who were continually unable
to recognize what was good.

Yet, without being asked, angels float bands of river
in the sky, tune forest skirling melodious.
In front of layered grottos of mud and vines
they can see panoramas shimmer sacred and profane.

They look toward the past: antiquity, extinction.
The future is behind, inscribed with feathers,
the script indecipherable.

We are surrounded with representations of angels,
awake or in dreams, as taught by religions or history;
by what we see in shops or even restaurants. We digest them,
sometimes seasonally, without too much thought.
Some of us feel apprehensive, some changed
in the presence of these angels. Though seldom
consulted, they are often ignored.

An angel falls out of a book, then disappears
from the room where the book, as yet unread,
is still being written. The book lies open
at the angel's page, waiting for chaos, or a carpet;
waiting for syntax, waiting for words
as yet unknown, waiting conceivably for wisdom.

After Paradise

Remembrance is the only paradise out of which we cannot be driven away.

— Jean Paul Richter

The Last Annual Death Party, by Invitation Only

Ferry ride at sunset to an island, long walk over night grass
to a fire already lit near sand, in the presence of water.
Our summer bodies circle the burning. Someone draws arcs
in the dark air above our heads with incense and Tibetan bells
and then around the jade-red glow of our collective nadir.

We ask the fire to take what we no longer want or need:
letters of termination; noise; photographs and diary pages
detailing the disintegration of relationships; weapons,
none too large; an empty picture frame whose splinters
the fire accepts more willingly than paper memories
or a diseased apple bough carrying the night chants
of a paranoid city neighbour.

A woman, Yarrow, sacrifices long thick ropes, knotted once
for each lover. Another offers cookies around the circle
before she tosses them. Their sweetness is immediately consumed.
Someone donates plastic high-heeled sandals and miniature tiaras
belonging to a brainwashed Barbie, then halter tops,
assorted sequin bikinis, a swath of platinum hair.
And afterwards the politically incorrect Barbie body naked
but for permanently sprayed-on lace-effect underwear.

A man called Forest wants to know, standing here,
which side of the last annual death party we're on anyway,
whether or not we're already there.

A paper watch enters the flames. The watch,
representing wasted time, is followed by money.
The money is also paper which means it's real.

When we can't think of anything else to throw
at the fire, we roast vegetables and render a version
of the Cherokee corn dance. The women among us
wear crowns of lakeweeds woven with late-summer flowers.
Small whirlwinds spin out over the peaceful altar of ash.

The lid of night lifts while we gather miniature baskets
of light, pour the sunrise into rice-paper boats,
launch onto the indigo inlets of morning
a flotilla of offerings — and post death-party hopes.

Cottage Plots on Posthumous Lane

for Ellis Peters, Ian Fleming, Ted Allbeury, Agatha Christie,
Dorothy Sayers and George Thorman

The Heretic's Apprentice drinks *A Rare Benedictine*
in *The Potter's Field* to mark *The Will and Deed*. He's known as
The Hermit of Epton Forest when he wears a *Monk's Hood* and holds
a *Dead Man's Ransom*. There was *One Corpse Too Many*
at *St. Peter's Fair*. With the *Flight of a Witch*
to a *City of Gold and Shadows*, *The Piper on the Mountain* found
The Virgin in the Ice. *A Morbid Taste for Bones* stains
her *Death Mask*. She's the *Holy Thief, Fallen into the Pit*.
During *The Confession of Brother Halium*, *Death
and the Joyful Women* dance a *Mourning Raga*
at the *Funeral of Figaro*. They sing: *Black is the Colour
of My True Love's Heart*. They return to a *Sanctuary of Sparrows*.

You Only Live Twice says *The Man with the Golden Gun*.
Live and Let Die at *Casino Royale*. *The Spy Who Loved Me*
had a *Goldfinger* and knew *The Diamond Smugglers*. *Diamonds
are Forever, On Her Majesty's Secret Service. From Russia
with Love* the *Moonraker* throws a *Thunderball*.
For Your Eyes Only, Dr. No.

All Our Tomorrows are a *Shadow of Shadows*, says
The Man with The President's Mind. But this is
A Time without Shadows when *A Wilderness of Mirrors*
reflects *Deep Purple*.

Three Blind Mice: Spies Among Us at *Philomel Cottage*.
Elephants Can Remember A Pocket Full of Rye with
*Surprise Endings, Starring Miss Marple. By the Pricking
of My Thumb* a *Third Girl in the Curtain* knows
the *Secret of Chimneys. Why Don't They Ask Evans? The Clocks*

are *The Moving Finger* in your *Ordeal by Innocence*. There's been
a *Disappearance of a Scientist* reported
by *The Woman on the Stairs*. *Hickory Dickory Death*
during an *Endless Night*. Throughout the *Crooked House*
The Pale Horse and *Remembrance*, of the *Golden Ball*.
Sparkling Cyanide, in a *Spider's Web*, hid
The Secret Adversary. *The Mirror Crack'd from Side to Side*.
A Murder is Announced. After the Funeral we're not
At Bertram's Hotel using *The Mousetrap*.
Remember the *Hallowe'en Party*? *Absent in the Spring*
The Five Little Pigs are more than a *Triple Threat*.
Witness for the Prosecution, and *Then There Were None*.
Thirteen for Luck, and *Black Coffee*, a *Cat Among the Pigeons*,
as well as *Cards on the Table*. *The Man in the Brown Suit*,
Destination Unknown, Remembered Death
in *The Hollow*, between *The Rose and the Yew Tree*.
For *The Postern of Fate There is a Tide, Towards Zero*,
as *The Unexpected Guest* considers *The Thirteen Problems*.
There's been a *Murder in our Midst*, a *Murder with Mirrors*.
Death Comes as the End, in *Nemesis*.

Strong Meat, Strong Poison, bring *Unnatural Death*.
The Nine Tailors, in *The Teeth of the Evidence*,
dress *The Five Red Herrings*. According to *The Mind of the Maker*
The Man Born to be King knows *Crime on the Coast*
through *Double Death*. Without *Clouds of Witness* he admires
Unpopular Opinions and can perform *The Song of Roland*.
Love All, he sings, it's a *Gaudy Night*. *Whose Body*
during the *Hangman's Holiday*? *Have His Carcasse* anyway.
Creed or Chaos, what's *The Scoop*?

Your Father's Gun

You're recalling the house of your childhood. It is empty.
You enter, run up the back stairs. You remember
a gun made by your father, kept in a drawer.

The drawer is there, waiting. First you notice
three hand-tinted photographs and a small velvet bag.
Then the gun. Its barrel is wrapped in translucent skin.

You sit at the top of the stairs, looking at a picture
of yourself as a child staring out through dark glasses.
Your hair is braided; your lips are too red.

And there you are again, at a table in a garden under
a willow tree. The mouth of the gun appears as a dark centre
among flowers. Your father is lunching with angels.

Like petals from flowers hung upside down to dry
too many faces are pressed together in this photograph.
There's been a parade, or a forced march.

In the small velvet bag you expect marbles: cats' eyes, puries,
clearies, boulders. You are disappointed by the old coins.
They are quite large, and flat: copper, silver, gold.

Some of the profiles they carry are blurred, a few
of the heads crowned with tines. These faces,
and the engraved surface phrases, are meant to reassure.

You hear a door close; another opens. The keys
remain in your hand. You put the coins back in the bag —
purple with gold braid — then the bag in the drawer.

It's your brother. He's wearing a belt woven
from claws and from horn. He looks at you then at the gun.
Along with three photographs and a bag of coins your father's gun

has lain for more than a decade like unworn underwear.
You already know your brother won't tell how best to use
the photos or coins or the gun, especially not the gun.

The trigger is still. You unwrap the skin
that covers the barrel. The skin yields, begins
to regenerate under your touch, slowly regains its own shape.

A young antelope stands beside you, flank attached to the barrel
of the gun. You are angry and demand that your brother release
the antelope's spirit, somehow confined for so many years

within the horn ornaments around his waist. And then
through the empty house *andantino* you perform a dance of antlers.
In the overgrown garden a water drum beats.

It would take a journey through afterworlds to join those garden
faces pressed into the photograph you found in a drawer.
You won't need anyone's gun or coins. And a gun, or an antelope,

wouldn't help in understanding your father
at lunch in a picture taken during the summer of angels:
a picture, turned so often in memory
by your no longer young hands, now dark, now scarred with light.

Misinterpretation of Dreams

Once we were women in Paradise.

> *Any woman in a dream indicates insincerity,*
> *bitterness, uncertainty, resentment*
> *whether she is young or old, ugly or beautiful,*
> *fashionably dressed or naked.*

We are naked because we've been in Paradise.
Now we exist to eat cookies. Most of them are round,
made from wheat germ and molasses,
decorated with candied fruit.

> *Baking is unpropitious: poverty and meanness*
> *can be expected, also ill health. The dreamer*
> *will bear much responsibility for others.*
> *Though a baker is a good omen*
> *whatever comes out of the oven*
> *portends the unpleasant and unpredictable.*

As the trays are removed from the oven
some of us think we recognize pineapple and apricot toppings.
The glazed cherries are in three colours.

> *To see or touch such fruit signifies*
> *an uncertain future and not much pleasure.*
> *Though eating fresh cherries may denote good health,*
> *picking them from the tops of cookies*
> *can lead to boredom and even dissatisfaction.*

We are being fed cookies by a creature whose hair
is the colour of sugar and whose brain knows how transfixed
we are by the batter of the afternoon.

To argue with such a woman foretells
the outwitting and outfoiling of the dreamer.

When sugar appears, there may be genuine worries,
bitterness, oppression. Both strength and temper
will be taxed. The dreamer is hard to please
in domestic situations, and seeking satisfaction
will find jealousy instead.

White hair is rivalry, or contagion,
perhaps calamity and grief.
A brain requires much caution.

No ordinary brain conceived these cookies.
Although they are our sustenance, we seem to be their pleasure.
There is some kind of bioelectronic connection between us
and them. They command us where to go, and how;
what to do; and then retrack, replay, rewind, erase.

Yet we can't live without the aroma of these hot cookies
and their soft skins that crumble between our teeth,
that yeastiness that seals us with desire.

Heat is not a very favourable symbol: it denotes
failure to follow through due to impending betrayal,
pressing financial need, a worrying physical weakness
and profound but short-lived emotion.

Sweet heat is even less favourable
especially if body parts are involved:
the dreamer's imagination is out of control.

Imagined, or real, a journalist arrives.
We register about as much optimism as there is salt
in a single cookie. And then she exposes her teeth,
prepared to bite. We're afraid she'll dip
those potential words of hers in honey.

> *If she is a journalist with a daily*
> *the dreamer should not be misled by appearances.*
>
> *Salt is an omen of discordant surroundings.*
> *Dissatisfaction will be everywhere*
> *and everything could go awry. The dreamer*
> *is downcast by a series of errors.*
>
> *Although honey is generally an optimistic sign*
> *its appearance could foretell unlawful*
> *gratification as fulfilment of desire.*
>
> *An ordinary dream of teeth augurs unpleasantness*
> *when in contact with sickness or the disquieted.*
> *Any examination of teeth is a warning*
> *to take precaution against those who lurk nearby.*

I'm trying to recall an old TV show where, to protect themselves
from the enemy, androids and clones exchange thoughts
through processed embryos. They must have been in
a parallel or malignant universe. Real thought is very difficult
for someone whose ideas are being controlled by cookies.

> *These symbols are beyond interpretation.*

Now the baker is about to disclose additional ingredients
to the journalist, including information about hermetic eggs.

Such eggs denote loss of property, and degradation.
If not thus already, whatever transpires
will not be in favour of the dreamer.

We see the swollen oval of an eye, a mouth moving
below a cheek inlaid with candied cherries.

To see an eye in a dream warns of watchful enemies
ready to inflict injury. If only one eye is seen
the dreamer will be threatened with loss and trouble
beyond which there is nothing more to imagine.

A woman's face signifies doubts and worries
now and in the future. Disfigurement signifies trouble,
the close presence of enemies, and misfortune.

I long for a future on a planet without cookies.
Can the journalist read between raisins and apricots,
pineapples, lemon rinds and three kinds of cherries?
In other words, will she be able to save us?
Or will she proceed historically, against intuition,
and just take fresh hot samples back to a megalopolis,
hungry to create an agenda of cookies for citizens
eager to be fed whatever their baker wants them to know?

To dream of a megalopolis indicates
ambitious ideals as well as sorrowful occasions.

To dream of a baker in a bake house portends assault.

To dream of a planet — with or without cookies —
foretells discovery, discomfort, unpleasant journeys,
and more dreams.

The Gathering of the Light

Though dark with swords and blood and mystery
in fairytales we read of sacred groves
mottled with hope and possibility.

Between the oaks, high elms and maple trees
ropes of arguing water pause then flow
quite dark with swords and blood and mystery.

The forest waits with quiet memory
for you there to find yourself, for you to know,
mottled with hope and possibility.

Ask the water, rising mist of history
why you can't stay; how, after here, you go
now dark with swords and blood and mystery.

Gather light from the river and the leaves,
small oracles as through the wind they blow
mottled with hope and possibility.

At dawn we watch you go, cartography
of argument, regret and peace, those groves
still dark with swords and blood and mystery
mottled with hope and possibility.

From this Time Forth and Forever

The glow of the sun and the moon and the stars
disappeared with the unravelling
of celestial harpstrings into shadow.
Then darkness sheltered in the umbra of your eyes

And death was your interpreter,
from this time forth and forever.
Your life was a tapestry, threaded with hope
and happiness and the colours of pain, and desire.

Our lamentations — mixed with laughter —
slowly gather into the fibres
of remembrance. Yet laughter is always heard
further than weeping.

With us are family and friends
who stood parallel, in rows,
as we left your grave,
plucking our few knots of grass.

We pour water over our hands, each one
setting down the pitcher, just as
we shovelled the earth, disconnected:
may the loss that began with your death there end.

We sit next to the ground, dust
on our feet and in our hair. We have ripped
our clothes instead of gashing ourselves,
counting your good deeds by our tears.

During the meal of condolence we are silent
as boiled eggs sealed inside their shells. Mouths
close around lentils that turn over in throats:
small, endless wheels of joy and of sorrow.

Our grief ripples into the concentric circles
formed by a stone flung onto water.
In the flame of the candle nearby: illumination
your wisdom brought to our lives.

Do not look for your body's reflection
in these mirrors, so recently covered.
Perhaps it is only such glass
that separates our worlds.

Let us offer a prayer brought by angels,
as the weave of your life is now spun
into the memory of children, bearers of your dreams,
from this time forth and forever.

After Paradise
for Bill and Vina Percy

In roadside orchards strung with yellow apples
undressed branches cross the autumn sky.

On trimmed lawns, life-size ornaments: Sylvesters, Tweetie
Birds, geese, pandas, Snow Whites and the Virgin Mary.

Chrysanthemums bloom on a terrace above graves
whose curved markers are stone fingers scratching.

From somewhere a *koto;* its translucent hum
summons spirits onto a burnished trellis of rain.

Home baking and watch repairs thrive behind double ferns
and prayer plants. Under a bird feeder's red roof, a well.

Clerics in collars and robes head for the salt marsh where
a prayer book society will rewrite the Scriptures.

Their daughters are all called Rebecca, Sarah, Rachel.
They are looking for birds to place on long, polished tables.

In someone's garden a pheasant calls out to the ground.
Crows sit on porches and carved balustrades.

At Victoria Beach, there is no longer sand or bathers
only docks with shellfish remains, dulse and gulls.

Steps from the wharf vanish with the quiet tide.
Here dolphins are known to swim unseen.

Dressed in orange waders, fishermen cast lots from boats
in shallow water. They lasso a wandering fish box.

On a steep slope behind them one tamarack blazes.
A ladder of its bright leaves drifts to the ground.

Ghosts of the Pony Express visit Goat Island
then sift among covered bridges for words.

Apples are punctured with nails in cylinders,
crushed between wood slats, strained for cider or wine.

At the edge of a garden a jury of cabbages
and pewter cages passes its verdict on the weather.

A pale company of hills washes the horizon with stone
in waves that are forever, though often veiled.

Inside your house there is cranberry glass and
a Crown Brand Extracts clock, once from Montreal.

Brown and silent, its hands on a staircase wall
are keys to a world beyond illness and coughing.

The black stove with doors of glass and gold
vibrates like a *shakuhachi*, watery with breath.

There is a dog in the red-roofed doghouse
on a lump of its very own land in a pond.

A propeller was once found in a field, nothing else.
A gospel lighthouse stands there now, open for prayer.

Behind shutters, under gables: wool yarn and
pear jelly, berry vinegar are often for sale.

All night daggers from across the river light the water
between these shores. The moon pulls. Nothing moves.

In the morning the air has the sheen of new wheat,
the sound of honey. It feels like the ripeness

of apples in the orchards after Paradise, or the sun
in the doorway your beloved is holding between her hands.

Photo by Julia Seager

Janis Rapoport's award-winning poetry has appeared in many publications both in Canada and abroad, most recently in *Border Lines,* the new international anthology of English-language poetry and in French translation in the Paris-based journal *Europe.* She also writes short-fiction and drama, and is currently teaching at the University of Toronto's School of Continuing Studies.